The Ghostly Tales of Lawrence

Published by Arcadia Children's Books
A Division of Arcadia Publishing
Charleston, SC
www.arcadiapublishing.com

First published 2022

Manufactured in the United States

ISBN 978-1-4671-9883-7

Library of Congress Control Number: 2022933025

All images used courtesy of Shutterstock.com.

Adapted from *Haunted Lawrence* by Paul Thomas

arcadia
CHILDREN'S BOOKS

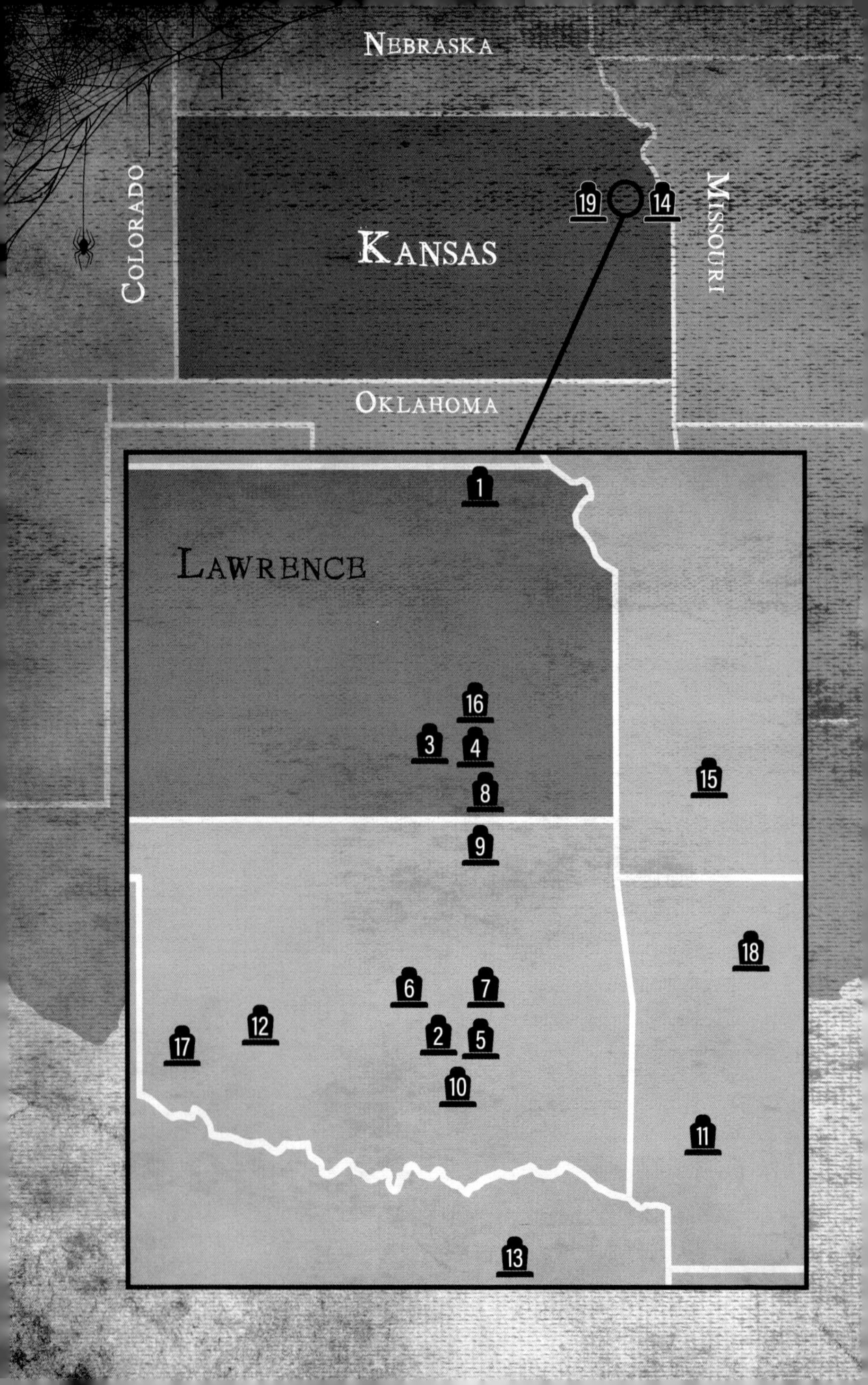

NEBRASKA
COLORADO
KANSAS
MISSOURI
OKLAHOMA
LAWRENCE
19
14
1
16
3
4
8
15
9
18
6
7
12
2
5
17
10
11
13

Table of Contents & Map Key

Introduction

Imagine what life would be like if you were alive in 1854. It was seven years before the American Civil War. People traveled in wagons and stagecoaches pulled by horses. Girls wore long skirts and boys wore short pants. You might attend a one-room school, or you might work on the farm or as an apprentice to a blacksmith or wagonwright.

Slavery was the biggest topic of conversation in the halls of government and in homes across the nation. Where could you go to support the anti-slavery movement?

You could settle in Lawrence, in the Territory of Kansas.

Today, Lawrence is a small city that is home to several world-class universities. But in the 1850s, Lawrence played a big role in the anti-slavery movement. It was founded by men who brought anti-slavery settlers to the Territory of Kansas.

Why was it so important to bring anti-slavery settlers to Lawrence? Because Kansas was not part of the United States yet. The people who settled the Territory of Kansas were going to vote whether to enter the United States as a free state or a slave state. Abolitionists (people who were anti-slavery) hoped to end slavery in the United States by having more free states than slave states in the union.

Lawrence sits on the banks of the Kansas River (also known as the "Kaw River"), a one-day horse ride from the Missouri border. Missouri was a slave state, and most of the people on the border with Kansas wanted it to stay that way. The border between the Territory of Kansas and the State of Missouri was often the site of conflict and bloodshed. It was a dangerous time for everyone, even children.

After many years of violent skirmishes, raids, and assaults between the Kansas abolitionists (known as Jayhawkers) and the Missouri pro-slavers (known as Bushwhackers), Kansas was admitted to the union as a free state in 1861.

But the border violence did not end.

In 1863, when the American Civil War was raging, a group of Confederates led by William

Quantrill attacked the city of Lawrence. The locals call the attack Quantrill's Raid. Quantrill's gang, which included Frank and Jesse James, murdered 164 people and burned the city of Lawrence to the ground. Quantrill and his men were ruthless. Most of the people killed were unarmed. But, the people of Lawrence did not give up. They rebuilt the city, which is still full of unconventional, fiercely independent thinkers. It is a hard place to leave. And many haven't, even in death.

CHAPTER 1

The First Haunts

Lawrence has seen its share of suffering and death, which has often led to ghostly activity. The city has a long history of strange phenomena. Lawrence has always been full of stories about noisy ghosts, haunted buildings, and spooky schools.

In 1885, the *Lawrence Daily Journal* printed articles about a haunted house that was attracting attention. Rumors spread throughout town about the ghostly happenings, and grown men challenged each other to spend the night in the spooky building.

Would you believe the eerie stories? Would you spend a night in the haunted house to find out if the stories were true?

Eventually, three young men took up the challenge to stay a night in the house. They boldly entered, burning matches to light their way. They laughed and joked with each other until suddenly, a full-bodied specter appeared before them! One of the young men drew a pistol and fired three shots at the ghost. Of course, everybody knows you can't hurt a ghost. The bullets had no effect on the apparition, and the men ran out of the house as fast as they could.

Where did this ghost come from and why was it haunting the house? The address of this haunted house has been lost in time, so we may never know. The *Lawrence Daily Journal* published another haunted house story in the early 1900s that had much more information. According to the article, a terrible tragedy occurred before the town was established.

The story says that Native American huts had been abandoned along the Kansas River, and a white trader claimed one as his home. He was a hefty, strong, intimidating man who made money trading goods. But he got greedy. He became an outlaw, stealing and murdering his way to a fortune.

Eventually, he traveled east and found a wife. But he didn't tell her how he made his money. He brought his new wife to his home on the Kansas River, and little by little, she learned how her husband made his living. The wife did not approve of her husband's criminal ways, and she came to reject him.

One night, the man led a raid on innocent people that ended in grisly murder. The wife was so disgusted, she decided to take justice into her own hands. She waited until her husband was fast asleep, and then she killed him in his bed. Afterward, she paced around the hut looking for a place to hide his body. Soon, the sun was coming up, and in desperation, she dragged her husband's body to the basement.

Many years later, a new family moved into the hut, and the haunting began. At night, the occupants heard restless footsteps stomping about the building as the ghost of the wife continually looked for a place to hide her husband's body. Every evening, the haunting ended with the loud, unmistakable thump, thump, thump, of a body being dragged down the basement stairs.

According to the newspaper story, more than one family experienced the ghostly noises. The story did not give the address of the building, but we can assume that it has been torn down and the vengeful wife is finally at rest. Or maybe she still roams the quiet streets of the neighborhood, looking for a place to bury her husband's body.

CHAPTER 2

The Ghosts of Quantrill's Raid

German immigrant Phillip Albach chose to move to Lawrence in 1858 because he supported the anti-slavery movement. Soon after his arrival, he built a house and settled in with his wife and his brother, George.

The Albach house is located close to the Oregon trail, which is a 2,170-mile-long wagon trail the pioneers followed west. If you were a pioneer going to Oregon to start a new life, you would have found very few inns along the way. People like the Albachs often welcomed visitors who were traveling the trail. One of those visitors was William Quantrill, who didn't tell the Albachs his real name. They did not know who Quantrill was or that he was not going to Oregon—he was planning a deadly attack on the city.

Because the Albachs were kind to Quantrill, he posted several guards on their home when the day of the raid came. He wanted to spare the Albachs from harm. But Quantrill lost control of his men, and some of them decided to loot the Albach home. They ordered the family to leave the building, but George was frail from tuberculosis. Tuberculosis is a contagious disease that leaves its victims weak and gasping for breath. Today, tuberculosis is cured with antibiotics. In the 1800s, tuberculosis was deadly. George was too feeble to walk, so the family carried him out of the house on his mattress. In the yard, while George lay helpless on his bed, Quantrill's men killed him. Then they burned down the house until nothing was left but the foundation.

When the violence was over, the Albachs rebuilt their home and lived there for many years. Some of them may still occupy the home today.

Many people, especially the current owner's children, have seen an old man wearing a white robe wandering the hallways. Friends who have spent the night have also seen this man, who they describe as "part of the house" and nothing to be afraid of. Most believe the man in the robe is George Albach, still in the nightclothes he was wearing when he was killed. George also protects the spot where he drew his last breath. A wall has been built on the site where he was murdered on his mattress, and when the current owners try to hang pictures on that wall, the pictures always mysteriously crash to the floor. Usually in the middle of the night.

The children of the current owners of the house have made friends with George. They leave him small gifts like chewing gum, and George usually stays quiet. Usually.

Many other buildings were burned to the ground during Quantrill's Raid, including the McAllaster house. Like the other resilient people in Lawrence, the family members quickly rebuilt their home. Over the years, the property changed hands many times and was even a boarding house. Then in 1993, a new owner bought the property, and the ghostly happenings began.

The first thing the new owner noticed was footsteps pacing around the front bedroom, but every time he rushed to investigate, no one was there. Next, objects would disappear. When the owner despaired of ever finding the objects, they would suddenly reappear in a different location.

But that was only beginning.

The hairs would rise on the back of his neck as strange shadows flitted around him. Orbs of light darted through the dark rooms. Overhead, loud crashes shattered peaceful evenings, but when the owner ran upstairs to investigate, nothing had ever fallen. And several times, his heart nearly stopped when he was startled by the ghost of a woman wearing a blue and white dress and a red corsage.

Others have also had experiences in the McAllaster house. A workman was nailing sheetrock on the second floor. He stopped to check his plans—but heard someone or something continue to hammer in the attic above. Suddenly, the hairs on his arm pricked up—the workman felt he was being watched. He abandoned his tools for the day and fled the house.

Another time, a young boy who was visiting asked, "Who are those people in the basement?" The owner was puzzled, because there weren't any people in the basement. At least, not any you could see.

Now the owner was sure his house was haunted. Ghost investigators were called in. The ghost investigators used their equipment to confirm many strange phenomena. They heard children talking when no children were anywhere near the house. They felt the unnerving presence of a man in the basement when the basement was empty, except for the investigators. They even claim to have captured the ghost's unearthly voice on an audio recording. Another investigator noted the strange smell of smoke throughout the house.

The ghostly odor of smoke made sense. After all, the house was burned down during Quantrill's Raid. But the owner found out another fire occurred in the home in the 1970s, when a woman died. An older woman who looked just like the ghost in the blue and white dress wearing the red corsage.

Unlike many structures, the Fuller-Woodward house escaped destruction during Quantrill's Raid. Raiders were on their way to torch the house when they were distracted by a runaway pony. They gave chase to the pony and never returned to burn the Fuller-Woodward house down.

But as early as 1884, the house was said to be haunted. By that time, the yard was neglected and overgrown. The porch banister sagged and the paint peeled. Superstitious people began to avoid walking past the house. The building was offered for rent, but who would want it? Would you be interested in living in a strange, spooky house that had a cellar full of miniature doors and secret spaces? Would you creak open the small, odd doors and shine your flashlight into the secret, eerie nooks and crannies? What or who would you find there?

After many years, a family finally moved into the house. The family knew nothing about its chilling reputation. But it wasn't long before they were frightened by strange noises around the home. The front stairs creaked under the weight of ghostly feet. The family was often awakened by the scraping sound of furniture being moved, though when they investigated, all the tables and chairs and couches were where they should be. One hot summer night, a young man of the family slept downstairs. He was soon woken up by a loud *bang!* on the floor right beside him. Had something heavy fallen? The young man got up to look—but there was nothing there.

If you lived in the house, wouldn't you start to wonder—should you be worried?

The people who lived in the house tried to look for answers. A servant told the family a tall tale about a man murdered in the home. The ghost was said to come back to look for his murderers. No proof exists of such a murder, but it turns out someone did die in the house during the American Civil War.

Lucy Woodward and her newborn child died in the home in 1865. Perhaps they never left.

If you walk past the house on a still summer day, you may see window curtains flutter when there is no wind. Peek at the porch and you may see a rocking chair tilting back and forth, as if Lucy is still comforting her newborn child.

HOTEL
HOTEL

CHAPTER 3

Hotels, Boarding Houses, and Apartments

Some of the most haunted places in Lawrence are hotels and homes that have been turned into boarding houses or apartments. People do not usually live in hotels, boarding houses, or apartments for very long. The joys, problems, and tragedies they experience in these places can linger long after they have moved on.

The Eldridge Hotel is a five-story, brick building that is considered to be one of the gems of Lawrence. It is named for Colonel Shalor Eldridge, who built the Free State Hotel that once stood on the spot.

Eldridge built the Free State Hotel in 1856, funded by the same people who brought anti-slavery immigrants to Lawrence. It was meant to house pioneers traveling west on the Oregon trail, but it soon became a haven for abolitionists. The pro-slavery people were worried about the growing number of abolitionists in the area, and they ordered the county sheriff to burn the hotel to the ground.

That didn't stop Eldridge. He built another, grander hotel on the same lot and called it the Eldridge House, but it was also burned to the ground during Quantrill's Raid.

Eldridge was not going to let the pro-slavery people ruin him. He did not give up. He built yet another inn, and in 1865, the Eldridge Hotel opened. Many have checked into the beautiful building, but not all of them have checked out.

When you visit, first take a look at the spooky photo at the front desk. In the photo you will see the elevator, open wide, and a misty apparition at the sliding doors. Many people believe the mist in the photo is the spirit of a former bellhop. Guests in the hotel often experience his presence as he performs his duties. He opens and closes the elevator doors and sends the lift up and down, even though the riders have not pushed any buttons. The ghostly elevator bellhop's most frequent destination is the fifth floor, which is the most haunted space in the building.

Before you take a ride with the elevator bellhop, be sure to request a stay in room 506. This room is considered the most active in the whole building because it contains the structure's original cornerstone. Many believe the stone is a portal that allows contact with spirits on the other side.

Keep your fingers crossed that your key card will work. Once, a housekeeper found that her key card wouldn't work. The manager at the front desk tried to use the housekeeper's key card, then tried to use a new key card, and then even made a new master key card to get into the room. Even though the lights flashed green on the lock, the door wouldn't open. Finally, maintenance people had to remove the door trim and take the door off its hinges to get into the room. They found that the dead bolt had been turned—but the dead bolt can only be turned from the inside. No one was in the room, so who had locked the door? Was it a ghost, looking for a little privacy?

The workers at the Eldridge Hotel have many strange experiences in room 506. Doors open and close all by themselves. Lights flicker. Strange, foggy handprints appear on just-cleaned mirrors. The director of housekeeping once stepped out of the room for a brief moment, and when she returned, all the drawers in the furniture had been pulled open. A valet passing room 506 heard voices coming from the room, even though no one had checked in. At least, no one who was alive.

But hotel employees are not the only ones who have had spooky encounters. Children who have stayed in room 506 report seeing full-bodied apparitions. One hotel guest who asked to be moved out of room 506 reported that as he was falling asleep, the bathroom door slammed shut. He got out of bed and opened it, but once he got

back in bed, the door slammed shut again. So, he wedged a towel in the door jamb to prop the door open and went back to bed, sure he had fixed the problem.

Slam! The door banged closed again, and when the man went to check, he found the towel had been removed from the door jamb and thrown in the bathtub by unseen hands.

He did not spend another night in room 506.

If you feel adventurous, steel your nerves and head to the hotel basement where there's a parlor called the Big 6 Room. Visitors have snapped eerie pictures of apparitions in this room. One teenaged girl captured a tall, dark figure standing in the stairway that leads to the Big 6 Room. The figure was solid, ". . . as if it was drawn on the screen [of the phone] with a Sharpie pen." The photo frightened the girl so much she deleted it from her phone.

In an out-of-the-way alcove in the basement, you will find Colonel Eldridge's chair. The chair is said to never collect dust—quite a feat in a musty storage area in a basement—and is said to be the center of ghostly activity.

A bellman once scoffed at the stories he heard about the chair, so he decided to have a look for himself. He went downstairs, unlocked the basement door, continued up some concrete steps—and suddenly broke out in goosebumps! Determined to overcome his fear, the bellman turned the corner, looked up at the chair, and saw a figure: A genteel, older man calmly sat in the chair smoking a pipe. He looked at the bellman and simply said, "Hm."

The bellman let out a bloodcurdling scream and tore out of there. He never visited the basement again, and yes, he no longer scoffed at the stories. Many other people have seen the ghost of Colonel Eldridge, pipe in hand, walking throughout the hotel. Stay alert, and you too will smell his tobacco smoke.

Like many older houses, the 1890 Goodrich house started out as a family home and was eventually turned into apartments. Many college students have lived in the house, and they have spine-tingling stories to tell.

First, people who lived in the Goodrich house regularly heard footsteps in a certain stairway, but it was impossible for anyone to be there—the stairway was boarded up! One occupant reported the eerie feeling that he was not alone in his bedroom. And one afternoon when a resident was alone in the building, the front doorbell buzzed and buzzed without stopping, as if someone were holding the button down. When he checked the front porch, no one was there. The resident grew annoyed and yelled, "Stop already!" The buzzing stopped. Then it started again. Every time the resident yelled for the buzzing to stop, it did. For a little while.

One snowy night, the resident was sure he heard someone walking around in the downstairs office. He was so convinced that someone had broken in, he called the police. The police came and found the office empty. There were no footprints in the snow, so no living person could have entered or left the office.

Doors slammed shut and locked themselves on their own. Lights turned themselves on and off. Phantom hands shoved residents in the hallway or grabbed their feet while they were sleeping. One of the occupants had an old sweater. The ghost would take it out of the closet and leave it folded on the banister for the owner to find. Once, a couple left their dog alone at home while they went out. While they were gone, something terrified the dog so much it tore through the screen of a second-floor window and leapt to the ground. He was sitting on the porch when they got back. What had frightened the dog so much that he jumped from the second story? What was he trying to escape?

Things got so bad friends refused to visit the people living in the apartments. Finally, a new owner bought the building and turned it back into a house for just one family. She sealed crystals and information about her family in the walls during renovation. It seems the ghost has been a little quieter since then, but that doesn't mean it's gone.

The Priestly house was built a year after Quantrill's Raid and is on the National Register of Historic Places. People who have lived in the house report it has a "creepy atmosphere," but one group of residents definitely had a run-in with a disapproving ghost.

A group of law students moved into the Priestly house and threw a party. They decided to play the song "Come on Eileen" on their stereo, but the CD wouldn't work. Every time the name "Eileen" was mentioned in the song, the stereo system turned itself off. After this happened five times, the group checked the electrical outlet and wires. Everything was in working order. The group decided they had a ghost and that the ghost did not approve of the naughty lyrics in the song. Or maybe the ghost's name was Eileen.

After that incident, the students began to have trouble with the washing machine. Once it finished its cycle, it would begin a new one and wash the clean clothes again. The students were sure it was the ghost, who probably didn't think their clothes were clean enough.

Later, the group found a treasure trove of glass-plate negatives in the attic. (Around the turn of the century, photographs were printed from glass-plate negatives.) They decided their ghost was someone they saw in the negatives: "a spooky lady [who] was real old, real skinny and wore a black dress." It turns out the lady in the glass negatives was Ellen Priestly. And the name "Ellen" is very close to the name "Eileen." Is it a coincidence, or is the building home to a disapproving ghost named Ellen? What do you think?

CHAPTER 4

Ghosts Around Town

Ghosts like to linger in homes and hotels, but they also like to hang out in businesses and other public places. One haunted place you can visit is Miller's Hall, a brick building just south of the Eldridge Hotel. Miller's Hall survived Quantrill's Raid, and its second floor became an unofficial town hall. Visitors included Carrie Nation, Elizabeth Cady Stanton, and Susan B. Anthony, who campaigned against the sale of alcohol and for the rights of women, and John Brown, the famous abolitionist. The building has housed several modern clothing stores. Employees have found objects rearranged by their resident ghost and doors slammed shut and locked. Some blame John Brown, but most say it is the spirit of Josiah Miller, who ran a jewelry store and a grocery store from the building when it was originally built. Perhaps Josiah is still busy tending the store.

The building that is now home to Vintage Church has housed many different congregations over the years. However, for three decades the Lawrence Community Theatre group performed there. During the theater group years, many strange incidents took place. Props frequently went missing. Stage lights would suddenly

stop working. Ghostly footsteps tramped overhead. Strange cold spots developed in several areas, and employees shuddered as they felt a "vague presence." The theater workers were convinced they were constantly being watched. An actress swore that she was pushed down the stairs, but when she turned to confront her attacker, the stairwell was empty. Bad luck also dogged the group. A fire destroyed two-thirds of the theater company's costumes.

In 1987, a set designer took a photo many consider to be proof that the building was haunted. Two actors were rehearsing onstage, seated at a table, and the set designer snapped a photo. When the photo was developed, there weren't two people in the photo.

There were three.

Standing between the two seated actors was a full-bodied, hazy apparition of a woman. The specter did not look like anyone who had been in the building at the time. Who was this spirit? Could it be the ghost of the person who owned the home that was knocked down to build the original church? Could it be a member of one of the many congregations that called the building their spiritual home? Perhaps she was a former church member, unhappy that her church was now a theater.

Most believe the ghost was a former church member, because now that the building has once again become a place of worship, the spooky activity has stopped.

Another very haunted place you can visit is Lawrence's Merchant's National Bank building. Built in the 1880s, the bank building is said to have been robbed by Clyde Barrow of "Bonnie and Clyde" fame. Today the spot is a popular restaurant.

When you come for dinner, ask for a seat on the second floor. But don't take the elevator. If you do, you might find yourself showered with an exploding light bulb, courtesy of the resident spirits. Take the stairs, but keep a sharp eye out. Many diners and employees have reported seeing a ghost going up the steps. Is it the spirit of a long-dead bank manager, securing the last deposit of the day?

When you excuse yourself to wash your hands in the restroom, be on the lookout. Don't be startled if you see the ghost of a woman in the ladies' room. Perhaps she's a bank teller from long ago, taking a break.

And while you're waiting for your

chicken fingers or cheeseburger slider, listen for phantom footsteps or the voices of those long passed echoing through the dining rooms. Footsteps and strange whispers are often reported by staff and visitors.

Even after you have paid your bill, don't relax. On your way out, you might see a man carrying a bicycle and dressed in clothes from the turn of the twentieth century. Can you feel the hairs standing up on the back of your neck? That's a sure sign that something eerie is going on. Don't try to chase the bicyclist—he will vanish!

The Merchant's National Bank building has been the site of many ghost investigations. One ghost tour operator spent a chilling evening in the building in 2011. She set up a laser grid on the stairway. If any otherworldly energy appeared on the stairway, it would interrupt the laser beams. This would show the investigator the shape of the energy. Sure enough, when the laser grid was turned on, a shadow person appeared at the top of the stairs.

The investigator also snapped a series of photos of a window. In the first photo, the blind is pulled all the way down. In the second photo, the blind has been raised two inches. And in the third photo, the blind is pulled all the way down again. No one had touched the blind—it had raised and lowered itself. Or did it have an unseen helper?

Don't miss exploring the C.J. Eriksen Building, the current home of The Toy Store. While you're looking over the merchandise, be aware that the resident ghost might be looking you over, too!

Employees of The Toy Store have had frequent encounters with their spirit. In the morning, they may find the basement lights turned on, though they know the lights were turned off when they left the night before. Strange noises are often heard in the store. Footsteps are heard on a certain staircase—but the staircase is between two locked doors. No one can get in—unless they can pass through walls. Shelves of toys and games might be rearranged. (Just think—the action figure you pick up may have been placed on the shelf by a ghost!)

The basement seems to be the most active area in the C.J. Eriksen building. Rotating book racks often squeak as if they are being turned, but when the employees investigate, no one is there. Perhaps it is a spirit who likes to read. Once, a worker found a single, muddy footprint in the middle of the basement floor. However, the floor had been thoroughly cleaned the night before. How had someone planted one muddy footprint on the floor without tracking mud all the way from the stairs? Another time, an employee was working late in the basement by herself. Out of the corner of her eye, she saw a black cat creep into the building through a pet door. But when she went to investigate, there were no animals in the room. She went back to work—and saw the black cat enter through the pet door again! She searched the room once more—still no cat.

The employee left the basement and finished her work during the light of the next day.

One truly astounding incident involved board games. The Toy Store employees were rearranging the store. They moved all the board games from the basement to the first floor. The next morning, the workers checked the basement and saw that all the Ouija boards had been removed from the first floor and taken back to their original spot, in the basement. This incident is truly spooky, because Ouija boards are used to supposedly communicate with the dead. Maybe the spirits decided they wanted to be left alone!

Who is haunting The Toy Store? Most believe it is Mathilda Eriksen. She was married to C.J. Eriksen, who built the building to house his furniture store. Mathilda was known to be an enthusiastic shop owner. Perhaps she too enjoys playing with The Toy Store merchandise.

CHAPTER 5

School Spirits

Most kids like going to school, at least sometimes. A school can feel like a second home to students, teachers, and administrators. But can you imagine liking your school so much that you never want to leave?

That's exactly what's happening at Lawrence's Cordley Elementary School, which was built in 1915. Cordley Elementary School was named after Reverend Richard Cordley, who recorded the early history of Lawrence and was an important citizen. The city was so thankful for his help rebuilding after Quantrill's Raid, years later, they named the school after him.

One ghostly student loves the school so much he is never absent or tardy. However, he is mischievous. Students and teachers report lights turning on and off by themselves, doors opening and closing on their own, toilets flushing when no one is near them, and footsteps echoing in empty hallways.

The spirit responsible for all these pranks is a small boy known as Tommy. Tommy moves things like markers, scissors, and books around the classrooms so the teachers have to search for them. Kids have even felt him tug their sleeves or push them. Once, a teacher witnessed a student's ponytail rise in the air as if it were being lifted—but no one was there.

Tommy has even been seen, and one custodian has seen Tommy *several* times. First, he saw a little boy running in and out of the gym, over and over. When he went to investigate, he found that the doors to the gym were locked. The little boy must have been a ghost who had run through the solid doors! Another time, the custodian was sitting on top of a desk in the gym. Tommy came up behind him, unseen, and pushed him off the desk. And once when the custodian was sitting on a bench and talking to a teacher, Tommy pushed the custodian off the bench, right in front of the teacher—twice!

If you have the chance to visit Cordley Elementary School, be on the lookout for Tommy. He is average height and has brown hair. You'll recognize him by the old-fashioned clothes he wears: dungarees (heavy-duty jeans) and a button-up shirt. Because of his clothes and his haircut, most believe Tommy is the ghost of a boy who went to the school during the 1950s. If you can persuade Tommy to talk to you, what secrets will he tell?

But Tommy isn't the only ghost at Cordley Elementary school. Keep a sharp eye out for a woman wearing a long, high-collared, black dress. She styles her hair in a neat bun on the top of her head. This ghost likes to glide around school, visiting classrooms. Usually, she stands in the doorway and watches what's going on as if she's making sure everything is in order. Students and teachers call her Hazel, because they believe she is the ghost of Hazel Lee Simmons, principal of the school from 1937 to 1965. Hazel is plain and serious, but not scary. When Hazel was alive, she was well loved by students and teachers, and she still is. Maybe she can tell you some secrets, too.

If somehow you miss getting a glimpse of Tommy or Hazel, you might see the ghost of Reverend Cordley, who is said to haunt the school. He wanders the grounds making sure things are running smoothly. Sometimes, when teachers are working late at night, they are startled to see him peering in the windows.

One more ghost has been glimpsed at Cordley Elementary School, but you may want to avoid her. On the upstairs level, a Lady in Red appears. She wears a red coat, but she is hard to get a good look at. She follows the living around, and they can only see her out of the corner of their eye. Some people say the Lady in Red smiles and is rather pretty. Others say they feel quite uncomfortable around her.

Another school, Kennedy Elementary, boasts a resident ghost. Kennedy Elementary

School was named after Opal Kennedy, a much-beloved teacher who taught for 50 years. She was thrilled to have a school named after her and in 1974 she said, "Now that was the greatest honor that has ever come to me, and I spent many hours and many, many times at that school. There are always very happy, happy, conditions."

Perhaps Opal was so happy at the school, she never wanted to leave. One teacher had a lengthy, strange encounter with Opal. The teacher had left some materials at school and came to pick them up over the weekend. While in her classroom, she heard a noise in

the hall. When she investigated, she heard rustling and saw a shadow disappear around the corner. The teacher followed. She walked to the corner, peeked around it—and saw the shadow disappear around the next corner. This time, she noticed the shadow was wearing a long dress, which was unusual for the time. Sure that she had seen another teacher, she found the custodian and asked who else was in the building.

He assured the teacher that they were alone.

She insisted, and described what she had seen. When she heard the custodian's answer, the hairs rose on the back of her neck. He laughed and said, "Oh, that's just the spirit of Opal Kennedy—she pops up every now and again!"

Some teachers are special. They want to nurture and protect their students.

Always.

University of Kansas

CHAPTER 6

Dorms, Libraries, and Fraternity Houses

The University of Kansas, established in 1865, is a seat of higher learning. Thousands of students have graduated from this institution. Many have lived in dormitories on campus or in sorority and fraternity houses close by. It is a great milestone when a student's years of hard work pay off on graduation day. Most graduates move on to fulfilling careers.

But some students don't want to leave.

Corbin Hall is a ladies' dormitory on campus that was opened in 1923. Corbin Hall has been the site of many happy times over the years, but it has also been the site of hardship. Soon after the dormitory opened, tuberculosis and influenza swept through the campus. The fourth floor of Corbin Hall was turned into a quarantined sanatorium to isolate the sick. A sanatorium is a health facility for people who have illnesses that last a long time.

Local lore says a murder took place in Corbin Hall. According to the story, one of the residents, named Abby, went to the basement to do her laundry. Unfortunately, a crazed intruder was hiding in the shadows. When Abby bent over her laundry basket, the intruder jumped her from behind, stabbed her, and left her for dead. Supposedly, Abby managed to drag herself from the basement all the way to her room upstairs where she scratched at the door. Her roommate, Sara, heard the scratching and instead of investigating what was making the noise, hid in her closet all night. When Sara opened her door the next morning, she found Abby in the hall, dead, in a pool of blood.

The problem with this story is it didn't happen, though people living in Corbin Hall sometimes try to spook each other by claiming to see Abby's bloody ghost. There are no records of any murder ever occurring at Corbin Hall, so you can be sure this is one of those ghost stories people tell each other for fun—that is, if you think bloody ghost stories are fun.

That doesn't mean Corbin Hall is ghost free. Credible people have reported strange happenings on the fourth floor, where the sanatorium was located. One college student was kept up all night when her door slammed shut over and over again. How many times would a ghost have to slam your door before you decided to sleep somewhere else?

Two other students decided to try to contact the other side through a Ouija board. They dimmed the lights in their fourth-floor room, placed their hands on the planchette (the marker that slides around the Ouija board and points to letters), and asked to talk to a spirit. After a while, they noticed a white orb hovering in front a mirror. Suddenly, the mirror fell and—*crash!*—shattered in a shower of glittering

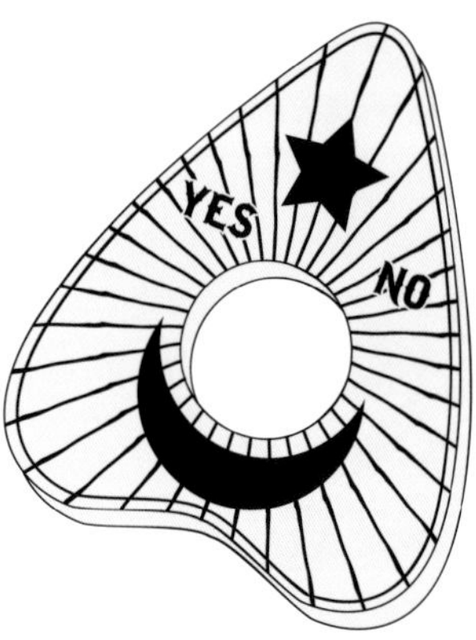

splinters! The girls believe they contacted the spirit of a long-dead resident.

If you're still feeling brave, you may want to visit the Kenneth Spencer Research Library, which is also located on campus. The research library houses collections of rare books and manuscripts. Some of the manuscripts date to the year 1000. The library even has a few clay tablets that date to 2000 BCE. With so many old books stored under one roof, it's easy to believe a few ghosts tagged along.

When you come, it might be best to take the stairs when you travel between floors, because the elevator is said to be haunted. Sometimes it has a mind of its own, stopping between floors and moving even though no one has pushed any buttons. Some believe the elevator is haunted by Kenneth Spencer, who donated his rare papers and books when the library was founded. Others credit Helen

Foresman Spencer, who personally supervised the remodeling of the library. Be sure to leave by the time the sun sets, because many report having an eerie feeling when exploring the stacks of old books at night.

Several fraternity houses located off-campus seem to have resident ghosts. The Delta Chi house is the home of a spirit who likes to steal keys. The ghost at the Beta Theta Pi house likes to flick lights on and off.

But the most intriguing stories come from the Sigma Nu house, which was formerly the Stubbs mansion. W.R. Stubbs was the eighteenth governor of Kansas. In 1907, he built his mansion on Windmill Hill, which had once been the site of a Dutch windmill. Stubbs and his wife, Stella, lived there. Everyone agrees that a tragedy occurred in the mansion in 1911, though the details are debated.

As the story goes, Stubbs fell in love with a teenaged girl whose name was Virginia. Some say Stubbs loved Virginia like a father—others say he was interested in Virginia romantically. He hired Virginia to work at the mansion as a maid. She was a friendly and reliable employee.

One day in 1911, after a long day working at the state capitol, Stubbs returned home and rang the mansion's doorbell. There was no answer. This was strange, because Virginia always answered the door promptly. Stubbs dug in his pocket and found his key. He opened the door, calling for Virginia.

No answer.

Now Stubbs became concerned. He looked for Virginia in the parlor. He looked for her in the kitchen. He even looked for her in her bedroom—maybe she was tired or ill? But she wasn't there.

Alarmed, Stubbs quickly searched the second floor and then proceeded to the third-floor ballroom. He raced up the stairs, threw open the door, and . . .

. . . there was Virginia. Her limp body dangled from the crystal chandelier—she had hanged herself.

Stubbs couldn't believe his eyes. As far as he knew, Virginia was a cheerful young woman. Stubbs continued searching the house until he eventually found his wife, Stella. She was sitting in a rocking chair on the rooftop balcony, in a daze.

Did Virginia commit suicide? Or did a jealous Stella decide to murder her?

According to the story, Stubbs committed his wife, Stella, to an insane asylum and had Virginia's remains cremated. He sealed her ashes behind a stone fireplace in the mansion. To this day, you can read the inscription on the hearth: "The World of Strife Shut Out, the World of Love Shut In."

In 1922, Stubbs sold his mansion to the Sigma Nu fraternity. The fraternity divided the house into bedrooms, including the ballroom where Virginia supposedly died. Reportedly, to this day, Virginia roams the halls of Stubbs mansion, lamenting her short life.

There are a few problems with this story, though much of it may be true. First, we know that someone did die in the Stubbs mansion in 1911. At the time, deaths didn't have to be officially reported, so we don't have any record of who died or how. Second, there is no record of someone named Virginia working at the mansion. But maids are people who are often forgotten by history—she may have existed, we just don't have any proof. Third, Stubb's wife, Stella, was never committed to an insane asylum.

But one key clue remains that supports the story. If you visit Sigma Nu house, you will see the strange plaque over the fireplace. When the fireplace was originally built, it was designed to be open on two sides: the entryway and the dining room. But the side that opened to the dining room was walled off and the plaque was installed sometime before the fraternity bought the house. Why? Many funeral directors have remarked how unusual it is to have a marker in a home that was surely made to serve as a grave monument. The plaque even has a panel at the base where loved ones can fill in the dates of birth and death.

The panel is blank.

What is hidden in the wall behind the strange plaque? For many of the fraternity brothers who have lived in the mansion, the answer is Virginia's remains. Because it seems that Virginia has never left.

If you spend any time in the house, you may hear her footsteps echoing in the hallways and on the stairs

as Virginia continues to make her way to the ballroom to end her life. You may encounter lavender-scented perfume, her favorite fragrance, wafting in the air.

Many people have witnessed the full-bodied apparition of a pretty young woman. She has been spotted staring out the window of the second-floor sleeping room. Sometimes, she is seen as a hazy figure wandering the bedrooms that were partitioned from the ballroom where she died. Other times, she is seen sitting on a stairway. She has even been known to open a closet door, float toward the bed where a fraternity brother huddles in fear, hover over the terrified man, and then return to the closet.

One year, the residents put on a silly skit at Halloween. One student pretended to be a ghostly Virginia, and the others pretended to "ghost bust" her, spraying the actor playing Virginia with "ectoplasm." Later that night, one of the partygoers asked the real ghost of Virginia to give the group a sign that she was present. Three beer bottles promptly exploded on a ledge.

If you visit the Sigma Nu house, be respectful. Because if you aren't, Virginia will let you know it.

CHAPTER 7

More Educated Ghosts

Lawrence is home to Haskell Indian Nations University, an institution that has the mission to educate students who belong to federally recognized tribes in the United States. Today, the university is a fully accredited, well-regarded school of higher learning. Unfortunately, it had a troubled beginning.

The school opened in 1884 as an industrial training school. It was meant to be a place where Native American children were trained to be productive members of mainstream society. Children, some of them quite young, boarded at the school, which means they lived there. They couldn't go home. They were taken from their families by force and compelled to give up their languages, customs, and religious beliefs. If a student did not follow the rules, he or she might be beaten, chained, and starved. The living conditions were brutal, and many students grew ill and died. These children were buried at the school, and many of their graves have been lost.

Over time, things got better. The students were treated more humanely. Eventually the school offered a high school education, and then college-level classes were added. In 1970 the school became a junior college and in 1993, a full-fledged university.

Considering all the suffering that happened in the old days at Haskell, it is no surprise that the institution is the site of many strange occurrences.

Built in 1898 and originally used as a chapel, auditorium, and then a gym, Hiawatha Hall is the oldest building still standing on campus. It is home to the ghost of a girl who drowned in a swimming pool inside the building. The pool has long been drained, but people who visit the building often hear splashing water. Custodians working in the building know to keep an eye on their tools, because the ghost likes to rearrange them or simply spirit them away so that they are never found! Hiawatha Hall is also said to be the home of a malicious, cloaked ghost who stays in the belfry and spies on people. And at some point in the building's history, part of the basement was sealed off. Some say the area was closed off to discourage ghostly activity.

Another spirit on campus, named Libby, haunts Tommaney Hall, which is the university library. She knocks books off shelves, whispers among the stacks, and flips the lights off and on. Students who decide to settle into a comfortable spot and read for a while sometimes get an eerie feeling, then notice a shadowy figure of a woman watching them.

Students and faculty sometimes note a ghost who hangs out in Haskell Auditorium. Dressed in clothes from the 1940s, this specter is often seen sitting in the audience enjoying shows that are staged in the theater. He seems to be a friendly, happy sort, but things aren't so pleasant backstage. Performers often report hearing the disturbing sound of someone crying.

Today's Haskell students coexist with yesterday's students who haven't moved on, even in death. Many current students report seeing late-night, full-bodied apparitions, feeling strange presences, or hearing children's footsteps. At Winona Hall, students often hear the sound of a bouncing basketball in the building—probably dribbled by the ghost of a basketball player who died while enrolled at the university. In another dormitory, residents often smell a favorite perfume worn by a student who died in a motorcycle accident.

Some of the most spine-chilling tales are told about Pocahontas Hall. Some stories state the basement of the building was used in Haskell's early years as a clinic for sick children, other stories say it was used as a morgue. Today, many claim to have heard the heartbroken sobbing of these poor children echoing in the building. Another story contends that a female student hung herself in the basement, and that on still nights, one may see the uncanny shadow of her body suspended from the ceiling.

Students at the school feel protected by the spirits of the children who died in the early years of Haskell's existence. They call these children the "Haskell Babies." The Haskell Babies are often seen around the area dressed in clothes from different eras in the past. They can also be heard crying on the Haskell Rail-Trail, which is a walking path built on the former railway that brought the first children to the industrial school.

Haskell Indian Nations University guards its resident spirits. Ghost hunting is forbidden. The faculty, administration, and students at the university respect those who have passed to the spirit world and treat them as equals. They refuse to exploit these entities, who they consider to be part of the university family.

Though it is located ten miles away from Lawrence in Baldwin City, we have to mention the ghosts of Baker University. Baker University was found in 1858 and is the oldest continually operating university in the state of Kansas. And the sight of many spooky tales.

One popular ghost story involves Parmenter Hall, which was built through private donations from many people, including Abraham Lincoln. In 1863, a Union soldier was riding by the area when he saw a bushwhacker posse—it was Quantrill and his men, who had just burned Lawrence to the ground. They were intent on dealing the same fate to Baldwin City. The Union soldier took off to sound the alarm, but the Raiders were on his heels. They murdered him on the new foundations of what

would become Parmenter Hall. However, the townsfolk noticed the commotion and took up their weapons. They fended off Quantrill and his men. When you visit, check out the building's tower. You may see the ghost of the soldier walking around it, watching for danger and ready to sound the alarm.

Rice Auditorium on Baker campus is an active site. Theater students often get the strange feeling they are being watched. Someone who is unseen moves props and tools from their resting places. Most believe it is the theater-loving ghost of Stuart McCoy, a theater major who died in a horrific fire in a fraternity house in 1976.

Finally, two ghosts are said to call the Old Castle Museum home. One ghost, Thomas, is thought to be a bit of a rascal. In fact, a retiring museum curator even left a note for his replacement that read: "Look out for Thomas." Be sure to charge your phone before you go, because Thomas is known to enjoy unplugging things.

The second Old Castle Museum ghost is more helpful. In one strange incident, a curator was carrying an armful of artifacts down the stairs. She tripped. She should have fallen to the bottom of the stairwell and injured herself severely, but instead, something—or someone—stopped her fall. The curator

believes this friendly spirit is a man who died at the turn of the twentieth century, crushed by an enormous grindstone that operated in the building at the time. Faculty members have even seen his face peering out a window late at night, when the castle is locked and empty. If you time your visit just right, maybe you will see him, too.

CHAPTER 8

Down by the River

Most paranormal investigators believe spirits are attracted to water because water conducts energy. Many ghost stories take place near ponds, lakes, and rivers. And the Kansas River has its share of spine-tingling tales.

If you're traveling to Lawrence from the east, stop at the ghost town of Weaver. Weaver was located in Weaver Bottoms, an area in the Kansas River floodplain. The town of Weaver was wiped out by a massive flood in 1951 and nothing remains. Except the shrill wail of a ghost.

Visit this bend in the Kansas River at night and your hair may stand straight up as you hear the sad, heart-stopping scream of a long-dead mother, mourning her children who were struck and killed by a train. Try to stay calm as you drive away, but check your rearview mirror—you may see a weird apparition chasing your car. You have just encountered the frantic ghost-mother of Adam and Oscar Toye, two young boys who were hit and killed by a train in 1889.

At the Kansas River in Lawrence, many have seen the eerie apparition of Lizzie Madden. In 1897, Lizzie was found dead in the sticky mud at the edge of the Kansas River. At first, authorities thought she'd had an accident on the old Northwestern railroad bridge as she tried to cross the river. They believed that one of the crossties snapped under her weight, and she had fallen to her demise.

However, Lizzie's death was suspicious. Just weeks before, she had told the police about some men who were making illegal alcohol. The men found out, and they threatened her life. They said she would never live to testify against them. Was it a coincidence, or did these hardened criminals murder Lizzie? No witnesses came forward, so we will never know. But we do know that Lizzie is not at rest.

Only a few months after Lizzie's body was discovered, passersby began to report seeing an apparition on the bridge where Lizzie fell. Some witnesses said the spirit acted like it was in pain, others said it behaved like it was locked in a struggle, as if the ghost were reenacting its own murder. One man was so frightened by what he saw, he shot a loaded gun at the specter until the gun was empty. Many prominent citizens claimed to have seen the ghost, so the story was taken seriously. So many people came to see the ghost for themselves, the bridge had to be closed.

The railroad bridge where Lizzie lost her life has long been torn down, but people still claim to witness the phantom death-struggle of poor Lizzie Madden at the Kansas River.

You can still see what is left of an old pylon of the old iron wagon bridge, located under the U.S. 40 and U.S. 50 bridges. It is the site of another terrible crime: the lynching of Pete Vinegar, Isaac King, and George Robertson.

Pete Vinegar was the head of a poor family that was notorious in the Lawrence area for petty crimes. In 1882, Pete's daughter, Sis, made a plan with Isaac King and George Robertson. She would lure a wealthy resident to meet her under the iron wagon bridge where the two men would rob him.

Everything was going to plan. The wealthy man arrived under the bridge in the middle of the night, expecting to meet Sis. Instead, he was attacked by Isaac King and George Robertson, who beat him viciously with a hammer and crowbar while Sis begged them to spare his life. The two could not be stopped, and the man was beaten to death. A few days later, his corpse was found floating in the river.

There was no question that George Robertson and Isaac King were the murderers—Robertson had been bragging all over town about what he had done. The police soon arrested Robertson and King, but they also arrested Pete Vinegar.

Pete had not had anything to do with the crime. He was totally innocent. But he had a bad reputation in town, and he was thrown in jail with the true murderers.

The townspeople were fuming. How could an innocent man have lost his life to these killers? The citizens did not want to wait for a trial, so they broke into the jail, grabbed the three men, and dragged them to the iron wagon bridge where they had committed their crime.

Robertson, who had bragged about the crime he committed, now threw himself on the ground and begged for mercy. King and Vinegar remained calm. The mob hanged Pete Vinegar, Isaac King, and George Robertson in the middle of the bridge. They may have punished two killers, but they also took the life of an innocent man.

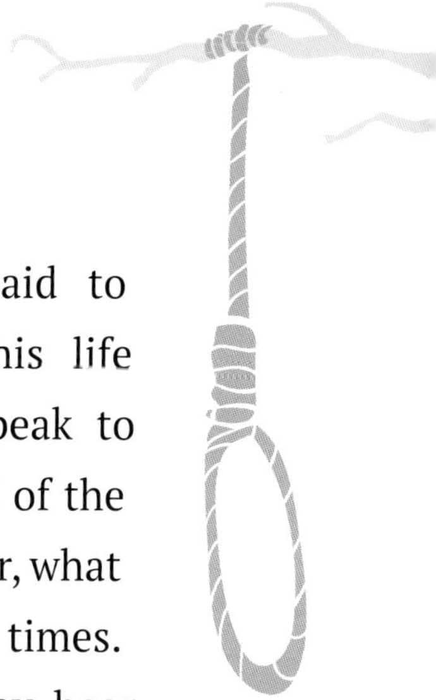

Pete Vinegar's ghost is said to still haunt the spot where his life was taken. If you want to speak to him, stand at the northern end of the bridges and chant, "Pete Vinegar, what did they hang you for?" three times. If you listen carefully, you may hear Pete's deep, unsettling voice answer, "Nothing. I didn't do a thing to be hung."

CHAPTER 9

Not-so-final Rest

The first public burial in Lawrence happened in 1854 when Moses Pomeroy died of the "Illinois fever." A farmer donated land on a grassy hillside for a public graveyard, and Oread Cemetery was established. Oread was the resting place for settlers and soldiers. Eventually, the victims of Quantrill's Raid were buried there in one, long trench. A few years later, most of Quantrill's victims were moved to Oak Hill Cemetery, and fewer and fewer burials took place at Oread. Eventually, Oread fell into disrepair.

In 1928 Oread Cemetery was renamed Pioneer Cemetery, but that did not bring the graveyard any respect. Tombstones were stolen. Unruly teenagers took potshots at the monuments. Cattle grazed on top of the graves. However, in 1952, the University of Kansas took responsibility for the cemetery.

Today, Pioneer Cemetery is in much better condition, but visitors report eerie encounters. When you visit, be ready for your cellphones and other electronic equipment to malfunction. But try to take a few photos before their batteries are completely drained. One ghost in particular may choose to make an appearance. He is a man wearing a top hat who walks among the tombstones, arms swinging. You may think you have met a historical reenactor, but if you catch him in a photo, look closely. You will see right through him to the dorm buildings in the distance.

Oak Hill Cemetery is the resting place for many people who are important in Kansas history. It has been called the Kansas Arlington.

Many report having strange feelings around a certain large mausoleum, as if they aren't alone. And if you dare, try to time your visit for the anniversary of Quantrill's Raid, August 21, when victims' corpses are said to rise from their graves and wander the cemetery.

Stull Cemetery sits a few miles west of Lawrence. A quiet graveyard in a sleepy town, Stull Cemetery has become the subject of wild stories and spine-tingling tales. Many have called Stull Cemetery the gateway to hell.

German-speaking settlers established Stull Cemetery near the Evangelical Emmanuel Church in 1869. Vague stories about the cemetery circulated over the years, but in 1965, visitors noticed something strange. An ancient pine tree, the oldest specimen in Kansas at the time, grew in the cemetery near the abandoned Evangelical Emmanuel Church. Over the years, the pine tree grew around a tombstone until it became a part of the tree. The tombstone stood over the graves of Bettie and Frankie Thomas, who died in 1879.

A story began to circulate that accused the two women of practicing witchcraft. The story also stated that the women had been executed by witch hunters, though no witch hunters have ever been reported in the State of Kansas.

During the 1970s and 1980s, more tales emerged about Stull Cemetery. Stull was said to be one of the seven gateways to hell, and somewhere in the cemetery, one could find a sealed staircase that supposedly leads straight into Lucifer's home. Some say the staircase is located in a burial plot, some say it is in a nearby field, and some say it is behind the chapel. If one can find the stairway and break the seal, time will speed up.

Many legends surrounded the ruins of the church. For instance, some claimed that if you drew an upside-down cross on a bottle and then threw the bottle against the wall of the church, the bottle would not break—or you better hope it didn't. If the bottle did break, the person who threw it would die soon. Others claimed that the walls of the old church bled when the devil visited, and that a cross bolted to the wall would turn upside down all by itself when visitors entered the ruins at midnight. In the 1990s, the roof of the abandoned church was blown away. After that, storytellers said that rain would fall all around the church, but never in the church. Today, all that remains of the church is a small pile of rubble. It was

demolished on Good Friday, 2002, because the locals were afraid it would collapse and hurt someone.

Why did the devil choose to make Stull a portal to hell? As you may imagine, there are many legends to explain the idea. Probably the most popular involves a tombstone that carries the name "Wittich." Some claim the devil fathered a child with a witch, but when the child was born, it was a horribly disfigured monster. The child was buried in the cemetery, as was his witch mother, who lies under the tombstone. According to the story, the devil returns twice a year—at midnight on Halloween and the spring equinox—to visit his dead son and his dead son's mother. And the devil installed a portal so he could get to the cemetery easily. But there's another version of the story: The devil's child did not die. He became a hound of hell, and he still stalks the graveyard during the full moon. But wait! Another tale says the reason that Stull Cemetery is a portal to hell is because a mayor was murdered in a barn during the 1800s. Supposedly, that barn was turned into Evangelical Emmanuel Church.

These are some pretty wild tales. Do you believe them? Many people do believe—or at least, say they do. The graveyard has been popular with high school and college students. They show up on Halloween in great numbers and leave litter, graffiti, and destruction in the cemetery. The sheriff has been forced to increase patrols in the area and impose large fines on those who trespass.

Some much more believable accounts of strange activity in Stull Cemetery have been reported by serious witnesses. Some visitors find that after a visit to the cemetery, they experience three- and four-hour lapses of memory. And one night, a university student and his friends investigated the graveyard. As the student walked across the uneven ground, he heard a noise behind him. Suddenly, cold fingers clutched his arm. He thought one of his friends had tripped and grabbed onto him for support, but when he turned around, no one was near him. His friends were twenty-five yards away.

Some ghostly tales are hard to believe. Other stories are more credible. So far, it is impossible to prove whether or not ghosts exist. Researchers can set up experiments, investigate sites, and catalog stories, but the best evidence will always be the incidents that you experience for yourself. Are ghosts real, or are they just stories?

What do you believe?

Lisha Cauthen lives in a 100-year-old house built on a Civil War battlefield and doesn't mind the phantom footsteps she hears in the attic. But she does get irritated when someone invisible blows on her neck. She is an editor and writes children's books including *You Are Here,* a nonfiction picture book about space. Lisha is a descendent of one of the Pilgrims, William Bradford, and many other immigrants who built new lives in America.

Check out some of the other Spooky America titles available now!

Spooky America was adapted from the creeptastic Haunted America series for adults. Haunted America explores historical haunts in cities and regions across America. Each book chronicles both the widely known and less-familiar history behind local ghosts and other unexplained mysteries. Here's more from *Haunted Lawrence* author Paul Thomas: